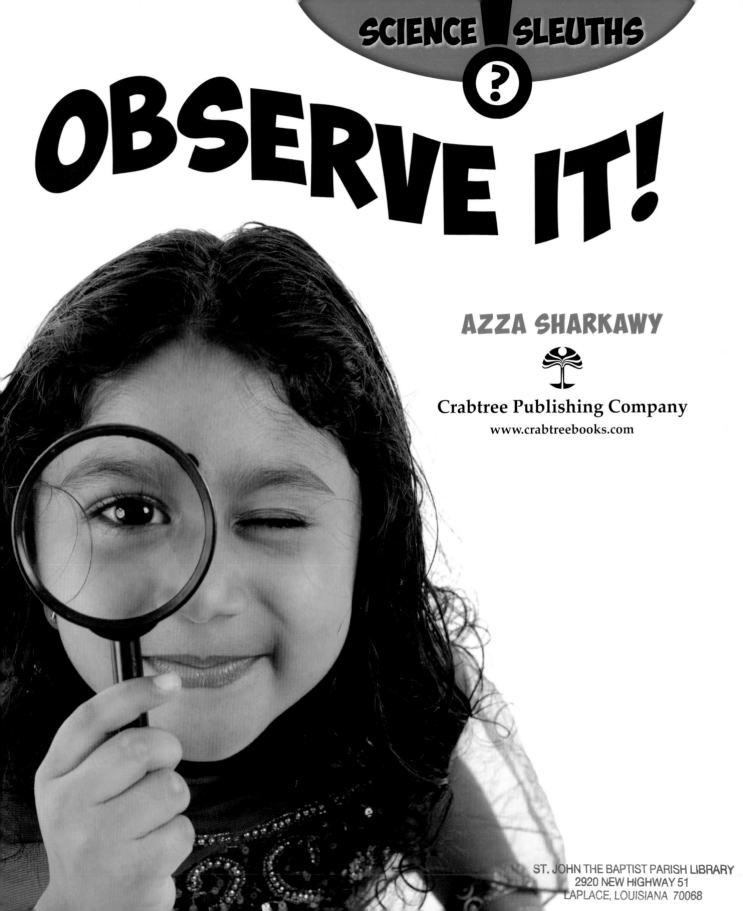

SCIENCE SLEUTHS

OBSERVE IT!

AZZA SHARKAWY

Crabtree Publishing Company
www.crabtreebooks.com

SCIENCE SLEUTHS

?

Author
Azza Sharkawy

Publishing plan research and development
Reagan Miller

Editors
Shirley Duke, Reagan Miller, Kathy Middleton

Proofreader
Shannon Welbourn

Indexer
Wendy Scavuzzo

Photo research
Katherine Berti

Design
Katherine Berti

Print and production coordinator
Katherine Berti

Photographs and illustrations
istock: p. 13 (left)
Thinkstock: Front Cover (diagram top right); p. 4 (top right); p. 15
Wikimedia Commons: p. 13 (bottom right)

All other images by Shutterstock

Library and Archives Canada Cataloguing in Publication

Sharkawy, Azza, author
  Observe it! / Azza Sharkawy.

(Science sleuths)
Includes index.
Issued in print and electronic formats.
ISBN 978-0-7787-0765-3 (bound).--ISBN 978-0-7787-0786-8 (pbk.).--
ISBN 978-1-4271-7712-4 (pdf).--ISBN 978-1-4271-7706-3 (html)

    1. Observation (Scientific method)--Juvenile literature.
2. Scientific apparatus and instruments--Juvenile literature.
I. Title.

Q175.2.S43 2014   j501   C2014-903938-7
                                       C2014-903939-5

Library of Congress Cataloging-in-Publication Data

Sharkawy, Azza, author.
 Observe it! / Azza Sharkawy.
   pages cm. -- (Science sleuths)
 Includes index.
 ISBN 978-0-7787-0765-3 (reinforced library binding) -- ISBN 978-0-7787-0786-8
(pbk.) -- ISBN 978-1-4271-7712-4 (electronic pdf) -- ISBN 978-1-4271-7706-3
(electronic html)
1. Observation (Scientific method)--Juvenile literature. 2. Science--
Methodology--Juvenile literature. 3. Research--Juvenile literature. I. Title.

 Q175.2.S528 2015
 507.2'1--dc23
                              2014032323

Crabtree Publishing Company

www.crabtreebooks.com   1-800-387-7650

Printed in Canada/102014/EF20140925

Published in Canada
Crabtree Publishing
616 Welland Ave.
St. Catharines, Ontario
L2M 5V6

Published in the United States
Crabtree Publishing
PMB 59051
350 Fifth Avenue, 59th Floor
New York, New York 10118

Published in the United Kingdom
Crabtree Publishing
Maritime House
Basin Road North, Hove
BN41 1WR

Published in Australia
Crabtree Publishing
3 Charles Street
Coburg North
VIC 3058

CONTENTS

EXPLORING OUR WORLD

How do ice cubes feel? What does thunder sound like? What colors are the leaves in fall? We use our **senses** to answer these kinds of questions. Most people have five senses. They are sight, smell, taste, touch, and hearing. Our senses help us explore and learn about the world around us.

We use our eyes to see, our nose to smell, our ears to hear, and our tongue to taste. We feel things by touching them with our skin.

Scientists use their senses to learn, too. Scientists are people who study the **natural world**. The natural world includes living and non-living things, such as people, animals, rocks, and water.

REMEMBER:

You must never smell, taste, or touch something if you are not sure what it is. It may not be safe!

5

OBSERVE WITH YOUR SENSES

To **observe** is to use your senses to learn more about things. Look for a rock outside. Pick it up. It feels hard in your hand. You might see dirt on it. You can see its color and shape. You are observing the rock using your sense of sight and touch at the same time.

WHAT SHAPE IS IT?

IS IT HARD OR SOFT?

IS IT ROUGH OR SMOOTH?

An **observation** is the information and details you get from using your senses. The more details you get by observing, the better you can understand something. Scientists use their observations to ask questions that will help them learn new information. They collect and record this information.

EXPLORE IT!

?

Look at the picture below. Which of the following statements is not an observation of this picture? Explain your thinking.

1. The bee is on a flower.
2. Bees make honey.
3. The flower is yellow.

MAKING OBSERVATIONS

Scientists make observations using one or more of their senses. Which senses could you use to observe this flower? What kinds of observations would each sense help you make? You could notice the color. You could feel the soft, smooth petals. The flower may smell good. These are all observations.

MY FLOWER

Sense	Observations
smell	strong, sweet scent
see	light pink petals, three green leaves on stem
touch	soft, smooth, silky petals
hear	You can't hear a flower!
taste	It is not safe to taste a wild flower.

EXPLORE IT!

?

Which senses could you use to learn more about an orange?

TOOLS THAT HELP OBSERVE

Some things are too small to see or too soft to hear using only our senses. Tools make what we are observing bigger or louder, so we can observe more closely and learn more information.

This boy is looking through a **hand lens**. A hand lens is a tool that makes things look bigger. It helps us observe things closely. Seeing things closely helps the children make observations with more details.

Some tools help scientists hear things that are hard to hear using only your ears. A stethoscope is a tool that helps doctors hear sounds inside your body, such as your heartbeat.

stethoscope

Some tools help us see things that are far away. Stars look small because they are very far away. A telescope is a tool that makes stars look larger and closer.

telescope

TOOLS FOR MEASURING

tape measure

Another way scientists make observations is by **measuring**. To measure is to find out the size or amount of something. Measurements are important. They give more details than observing with just our senses.

This scientist is using a tape measure to find out how tall the plant is.

We all use different tools to take different kinds of measurements. Rulers, yard or meter sticks, and tape measures are tools that can measure how tall or long something is. A balance measures how heavy something is. A thermometer measures how hot or cold something is.

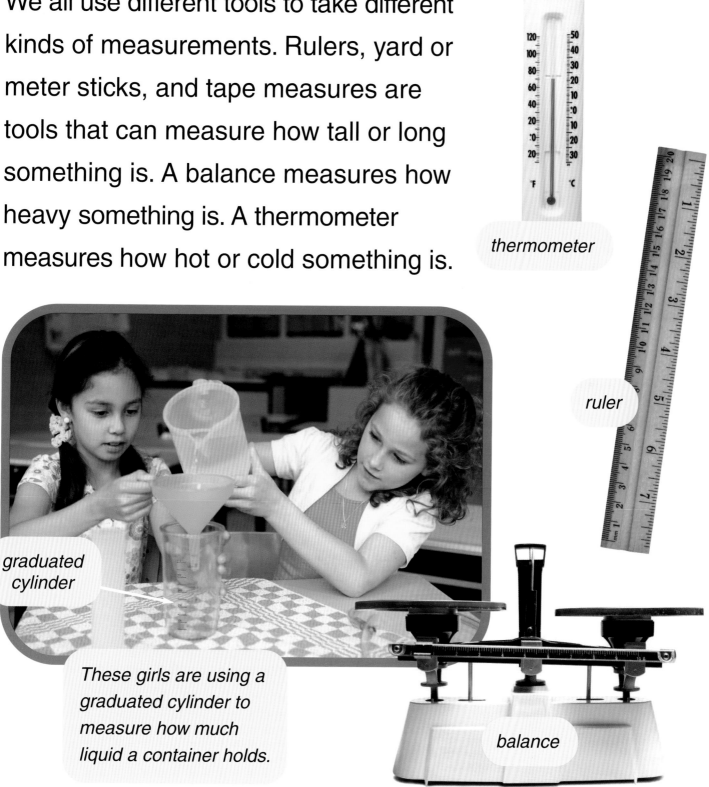

thermometer

ruler

graduated cylinder

These girls are using a graduated cylinder to measure how much liquid a container holds.

balance

RECORD IT

It is important for scientists to record their observations. They share the information they record with other scientists.

You can record your observations in many ways. Some scientists use pictures and words.

Dragonfly body parts

head   eye

wings   leg   thorax

abdomen

This boy drew a picture of a dragonfly. The labels name its body parts.

This girl is recording the weather by taking photos of clouds.

Some scientists record observations using numbers. Charts, graphs, and tables help organize and compare observations such as measurements. The girl below used a thermometer to measure the temperature in different places at her school. A bar graph makes it easy to compare these observations.

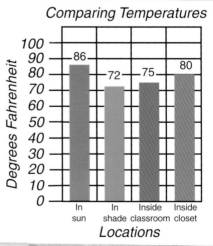

Comparing Temperatures

Degrees Fahrenheit

Locations: In sun (86), In shade (72), Inside classroom (75), Inside closet (80)

EXPLORE IT!

?

Look at the bar graph to find out the difference in temperature between the warmest and coolest places at the school.

IT IS ALL IN THE DETAILS!

Scientists are careful to make good observations. Careful observations can be checked by other scientists. A good record helps prove to other scientists whether or not the observations answered a question.

HOW DO YOU MAKE DETAILED OBSERVATIONS?

Take your time.

If it is safe, use as many senses as you can.

Ask yourself: What color is it? What shape? How can I describe its size? How does it feel? What sound does it make? What does it smell like? What does it taste like?

Use tools that can help you see closer up.

Use tools to measure.

Record your information as exactly as you can and share your observations.

EXPLORE IT!

Which observations are more carefully recorded? Why do you think so?

Data A:

6 legs, **2** feelers, **3** body parts, **2** eyes, brown body, one inch long

Data B:

legs, feelers, brown, and dark, little body

OBSERVE THE PROPERTIES

Objects have **properties**, or characteristics, that we can observe and describe using our senses. Properties are things such as size, color, weight, shape, and texture, or how things feel.

It is easier to describe and compare objects by sorting them into groups based on one or more of their properties. Grouping objects helps show how they are alike and different.

Rocks might be sorted by looking at their size or color.

Tree bark can be sorted by feeling how smooth or rough it is. Seeds can be sorted into groups using shape, size, or color.

EXPLORE IT!

Can you solve this riddle by the description of the mystery object's properties? What is black and white and round all over? (Hint: The picture gives you a clue.)

19

GROUPING AND CLASSIFYING

Scientists observe the properties of objects and ask questions to help **classify**, or group, them.

PROPERTIES

Soft
Heavy
Floats
Cold
Alive

EXPLORE IT!

?

Sort the objects on this page into groups by the properties in the list. (Hint: Some objects may belong to more than one classification.)

A magnet is a tool that attracts materials with iron in them. A property of some objects is that they are magnetic. That means they are attracted to, or will move toward, a magnet when placed next to one.

You can observe this yourself. Get a magnet and collect different objects from around your home. Choose ten objects, such as a ruler, a popsicle stick, a piece of jewelry, a shoe box, a mug, a piece of string, a spoon, a rock, a sheet of aluminum foil, a cork, or some paper clips.

Object	Magnetic	Not Magnetic

EXPLORE IT!

?

Hold the magnet next to each object one at a time. Observe whether or not they attracted to the magnet. Then record your observations in a chart.

LEARNING MORE

BOOKS

Think Like a Scientist in the Classroom by Susan Hindman. Cherry Lake Publishing, 2011.

I'll Use a Hand Lens with My Friends by Kelly Doudna. Sandcastle, 2006.

Looking Through a Microscope by Linda Bullock. Children's Press, 2003.

We Have the Nerve, Now Let's Observe by Kelly Doudna. Sandcastle, 2006.

WEBSITES

Use your senses to observe what happens when you try the hands-on science investigations provided by this website.
www.jumpstart.com/parents/ activities/science-activities

This is an engaging video on how magnifying glasses help us make observations.
www.youtube.com/ watch?v=ig-conEjtco

Watch the fascinating videos on this website and list some observations you can share with a friend.
http://discoverykids.com/videos/

GLOSSARY

classify (KLAS-uh-fahy) verb To sort or put into groups

data (DAT-uh) noun Facts learned by observations

hand lens (hand lenz) noun A tool that makes things bigger, like a magnifying glass

measure (MEZH-er) verb To find out the size or amount of something by comparing it to something else

natural world (NACH-er-uhl WURLD) noun All living and non-living things in the world

observation (ob-zur-VEY-shuh n) noun Fact you learn using your senses

observe (ob-zur-VEY-shuh nz) verb To gather information using your senses

properties (PROP-er-teez) noun Things that describe an object, like size, color, weight, shape, and how it feels

scientists (SAHY-uhn-tistz) noun People who learn about the natural world

senses (SENS-uhz) noun Sight, touch, hearing, taste, and smell

A noun is a person, place, or thing. A verb is an action word that tells you what someone or something does.

INDEX